D

COMPREHENSION MATTERS

# Main Idea and Details

*Options*
Publishing
A Haights Cross Communications Company

**Acknowledgments**

**Editors:** Jeanne Payne, Renata Jass
**Senior Designer:** Deborah Diver
**Editorial Development:** Hudson Publishing Associates, LLC
**Design and Production:** Think Design Group, LLC

**Cover Illustration:** Craig Orback

**Illustrators:** Judy Love, Drew Rose

**Photo Credits:** 10: © Ron Chapple Stock/Corbis; 13: © Viktor Korotaye/Corbis;
14: Punchstock; 17: © Ryan Mcvay/Getty Images; 22: © Jennie Woodcock/Corbis; 25: iStock;
26: © Annie Griffiths Belt/Corbis; 29: © Roger Tidman/Corbis; 34: © China Daily/Corbis;
37: © Robert Dowling/Corbis; 37: Corbis; 42: © Anthony Bannister/Corbis; 45: © Ted Horowitz/
Corbis; 46, 54: © Michael Newman/PhotoEdit; 49: Corbis.

ISBN 10: 1-60161-153-6
ISBN 13: 978-1-60161-153-6

Printed in the U.S.A.
15  14  13  12  11  10  9  8  7  6  5  4  3  2


Options Publishing
P.O. Box 1749
Merrimack, NH 03054-1749
Toll Free Phone: 800-782-7300
Toll Free Fax: 866-424-4056
www.optionspublishing.com

# Contents

# Identifying the Main Idea

To better understand what you read, you need to be able to identify the main idea. The **main idea** is what a story or article is mostly about. You can often find clues to the main idea in the title or at the beginning or end of the selection. Sometimes you may not find the main idea in one sentence in the selection. You will need to infer what the selection is mostly about. Read the selection.

## Michele's Aquarium

I finally have an aquarium! It's a pretty large tank. So far, I only have one fish, but it's a start. Mrs. Abernathy, the pet shop owner, knew I wanted an aquarium. She told me she was ready to replace a shop aquarium. Then we agreed I would earn it by helping her in the shop. It became my job to feed and water the animals. Three months later, the aquarium was mine! Dad helped me take it home. That night, my brother and I set it up. We put two rock caves in it. I added a treasure chest that opened and closed with the air pump.

I was imagining the aquarium full of graceful fish, when my cousin walked in. He brought me a gift! I noticed the pet shop bag. It was tied shut with colored ribbons. The label read, "Michele, Be Careful—Green Terror Inside!" With a label like that, I could wait to open the mystery gift. Finally, my cousin laughed. He said a green terror was a kind of fish for a large aquarium. The little bag didn't weigh much, so it couldn't be a giant fish. And it was probably harmless, too, right? Still, I untied the bag carefully.

**What is the main idea of the story?**

_____

In this case, the title, "Michele's Aquarium," tells us the main idea.

Each paragraph in a selection has its own main idea. What is the first paragraph mostly about? It is about Michele's aquarium and how she got it.

**What is the main idea of the second paragraph?**

_____

# Identifying Details

**Details** are pieces of information that tell about the main idea. They give you the 5 Ws and H in an article or story: **w**ho, **w**hat, **w**here, **w**hen, **w**hy, and **h**ow something happens.

In stories, details give you more information about the main idea. Details can tell you about the characters, setting, or events in a story. Read the paragraph again to find the details about the aquarium.

The details give you more information about the aquarium and the mystery gift. Complete the chart with the missing details.

| "Michele's Aquarium" Details | |
|---|---|
| **Who** is the story about? | Michele |
| **What** is the story about? | |
| **Where** does the story take place? | |
| **When** did she get the aquarium? | after working in the pet shop for 3 months |
| **How** does Michele get a fish? | Her cousin gave her the fish. |

Details in articles build on, or support, the main idea. They provide information about the topic and make the article more interesting. Read this paragraph. Find the main idea. Next, look for details that support the main idea.

## The Green Terror Fish

Have you heard of the green terror fish? It comes from South America. People with aquariums say it is easy to care for. The fish is oval-shaped and greenish-white. It also has a bump on its forehead. It can grow as long as 8 inches. So, the green terror needs a large aquarium. It got its name because it is always ready to fight. The green terror will attack and eat other fish. This proves that even a small fish can be a sea monster!

**List details about the green terror fish.**

_____

_____

# A Very Special Gift

Maya was excited about her mom's birthday. She was going to give her a special gift. Maya had thought about it for a long time. In fact, she had been thinking about it ever since Mom's last birthday.

Maya had two sisters. Last year, the other girls had given Mom presents. But Maya didn't have enough money for a gift. She gave Mom a card she had made. Mom had loved the card. But Maya still wished she had given a gift.

The next day Mom showed Maya a scrapbook. "I save important things in here," she said. The book had cards from all three girls. It was almost full, though. This gave Maya an idea.

She began to save money. Each week she saved part of her allowance. After a year her savings added up. Now it was time to give Mom the best birthday gift.

The next day was Mom's birthday. She opened many beautiful gifts. Then Maya handed Mom her gift. It was a new scrapbook. "This is such a lovely gift!" said Mom. "You remembered that my other book is almost full."

Maya also handed her mom a card she had made. "It was fun to buy you the scrapbook. But I know the cards you keep in it mean the most to you."

"You are right, Maya," said Mom. "Thank you!"

**What is the story mostly about?**

_____

# Multiple-Choice Questions

**1** **Another title for this article could be**

Ⓐ "Maya Goes Shopping."

Ⓑ "A Birthday Savings Plan."

Ⓒ "Family Party."

Ⓓ "Mom's Photo Album."

**2** **What birthday gift did Maya give her mother last year?**

Ⓐ money

Ⓑ a box

Ⓒ jewelry

Ⓓ a card

**3** **According to the story, what did Mom save in her scrapbook?**

Ⓐ photos

Ⓑ cards

Ⓒ money

Ⓓ letters

**4** **Which sentence best states the main idea of the story?**

Ⓐ Maya's mother made a scrapbook of all the cards she'd received.

Ⓑ Maya gave her mother a new scrapbook for her birthday.

Ⓒ Maya saved a little of her allowance to buy a card.

Ⓓ Maya's mother received many birthday gifts.

**5** **Why was Maya able to buy her mom a gift this year?**

Ⓐ She saved her money.

Ⓑ She asked her sisters to buy it.

Ⓒ She borrowed money.

Ⓓ She didn't give a gift.

# Short-Response Questions

**6** **Complete the diagram with two details.**

### Things Maya Does for Mom's Birthday

1. Maya saves money from her allowance.

2.

3.

**7** **According to the story, how long did Maya save her money?**

_____

**8** **Where did Maya get the money she saved?**

_____

**9** **Why was a scrapbook such a thoughtful gift?**

_____

_____

**10** **Why did Maya make another card for her mom this year?**

_____

_____

# Writing Connection: Nouns

A **singular noun** is one person, place, or thing. A **plural noun** is more than one. Here are some examples of singular and plural nouns.

| Singular | Plural |
|----------|--------|
| dog | dogs |
| page | pages |
| book | books |

1. **Complete the sentence with the correct noun form.**

   She was going to give her a very special _____. **gift, gifts**

   Maya has two _____. **sister, sisters**

   The scrapbook held _____ from all of her daughters. **card, cards**

   They looked at a _____ Maya drew when she was little. **dog, dogs**

   Last year, the other girls had given Mom _____. **present, presents**

   Maya didn't have enough _____ for a gift. **dollars, dollar**

   The next day Mom showed Maya a _____. **scrapbook, scrapbooks**

   Mom saved every _____ that she received. **card, cards**

   Maya also handed her mom _____ she had drawn. **picture, pictures**

2. **Write two sentences using singular and plural noun forms about Mom's birthday gift.**

   a _____

   _____

   b _____

   _____

# Therapy Dogs

Do you or someone you know have a dog? Does the dog help people in some way? Dogs can make great pets. They are usually loving, helpful, and loyal. Did you know that dogs can also provide therapy for people? *Therapy* is another word for *healing*.

The Delta Society and Therapy Dogs International are two groups that bring together people and animals. They train animals and their owners to visit schools, hospitals, and nursing homes.

Therapy dogs are different from service dogs. Service dogs are trained to meet the needs of people with disabilities. Therapy dogs provide people with animal contact. They are trained to visit with people. Owners of therapy dogs also go through training. It is important for the dog to listen to the owner and follow directions.

Therapy dogs and other animals can be used to visit people or to provide therapy. Visits usually take place in a hospital or nursing home. Some therapy dogs visit with sick or lonely children and adults. Therapy can take place in a hospital or a home. Animals can help improve the physical, mental, or social skills of people in need. Some of the other animals that can be used for therapy include cats, rabbits, and horses. If you do not have an animal, you can still be trained as a volunteer and work with animals.

One of the best things a therapy dog can give is love. Many people in nursing homes or hospitals are lonely or sad. Petting a dog can help cheer them up. Making a visit with a therapy dog is a great way to brighten someone's day!

**What is the article mostly about?**

_____

# Multiple-Choice Questions

**1** **Another title for this article could be**

Ⓐ "How to Care for Your Pet."

Ⓑ "Therapy Animals Cheer People Up."

Ⓒ "The History of the Delta Society."

Ⓓ "Therapy Horses Love People."

**2** **What are service dogs trained to do?**

Ⓐ provide people with animal contact

Ⓑ read with children

Ⓒ visit people in the hospital

Ⓓ meet the needs of people with disabilities

**3** **According to the article, what is one of the *best* things a therapy dog can give?**

Ⓐ time

Ⓑ love

Ⓒ money

Ⓓ peace

**4** **What is the last paragraph *mostly* about?**

Ⓐ therapy dog organizations

Ⓑ how therapy animals comfort people

Ⓒ how service dogs differ from therapy dogs

Ⓓ training for therapy dogs

**5** **Which of the details *best* supports the main idea in the article?**

Ⓐ A service dog may be trained to bring items to its owner.

Ⓑ A therapy dog may wear a funny costume for its visits.

Ⓒ Not all dogs can be trained to work with people.

Ⓓ A visit from a therapy dog makes people feel better.

# Short-Response Questions

**6** Complete the web with two details.

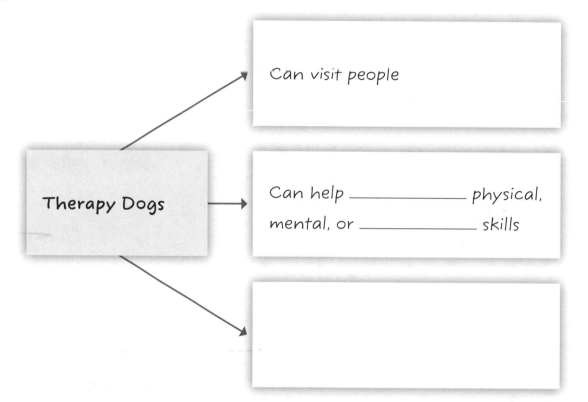

Therapy Dogs

Can visit people

Can help _____ physical, mental, or _____ skills

**7** According to the article, how are service dogs different from therapy dogs?

_____

**8** Name three places in which therapy dogs provide services.

_____

**9** After reading this article, write why making a visit with a therapy dog is a great way to brighten someone's day.

_____

_____

**10** List two therapy dog organizations.

_____

_____

# Writing Connection: Regular and Irregular Verbs

A **verb** is an action word. It can be expressed in many tenses, including present and past. Many verbs are expressed in past tense by adding "-ed" to the end of the word. These are regular verb forms.

| Present Tense |
|---|
| visit |
| train |

| Past Tense |
|---|
| visited |
| trained |

Some verbs are **irregular** and have different spelling changes in the past tense.

| Present Tense |
|---|
| bring |
| was |

| Past Tense |
|---|
| brought |
| were |

1.  **Complete the sentence with the correct past tense verb form.**

    The therapy dog _____ cheer up the little boy.  **help, helped**

    The trainer _____ the dog a command.  **gave, give**

    The people in the nursing home _____ glad to see the animals.  **was, were**

    The little girl _____ how to read better using a therapy dog.  **learned, learn**

2.  **Write two sentences with correct present or past tense verb forms about therapy dogs.**

    a  _____

    _____

    b  _____

    _____

# Bank on It!

Where is the best place to save money? In a piggy bank? Under a mattress? In a jar? While some of these places may work just fine, the best place to save money is in a savings account at a bank. The money will be kept safe and might also pay you for saving your money. Your piggy bank can't do that!

How can you earn money while saving money? A bank lends money to people and businesses. People borrow money for lots of reasons. They may need to fix up their house or help pay for college. Businesses borrow money to build new stores or to buy new equipment. People and businesses pay the borrowed money back to the bank a little at a time. They also pay back more money than they borrowed. The extra money they pay the bank is called interest.

A bank uses the interest money for many things. It uses some of it to pay employees. A bank also pays some of that interest to people who have savings accounts. The money the bank lends comes from the savings accounts of many different people. The bank pays them to use their money. This amount is also called interest.

You may wonder if your money will still be in the bank when you want to take it out, or withdraw it. Don't worry. A bank has to have cash at all times. This allows a bank to give people their money whenever they want it.

Money stored in a bank is very safe. There is a giant vault in a bank that is locked. There are also laws to make sure that a bank will return any money people might save with it. A savings account is a very good place to keep money. You can bank on it!

**What is the article mostly about?**

_____

# Multiple-Choice Questions

**1** **Another title for this article could be**

(A) "Visiting a Bank."

(B) "The History of Banking in America."

(C) "How a Bank Can Earn You Money."

(D) "My Piggy Bank."

**2** **According to the article, where does a bank store money?**

(A) in a piggy bank

(B) under a mattress

(C) in a vault

(D) in a jar

**3** **What is the first paragraph *mostly* about?**

(A) working in a bank

(B) places to save money

(C) piggy banks

(D) borrowing money

**4** **How does a bank use interest money?**

(A) to build a vault

(B) to give to colleges

(C) to buy piggy banks

(D) to pay interest to others who save

**5** **Which of the following is *not* a reason people might borrow money?**

(A) to throw it away

(B) to fix up a house

(C) to pay for college

(D) to pay some bills

# Short-Response Questions

**6** Complete the web with two details.

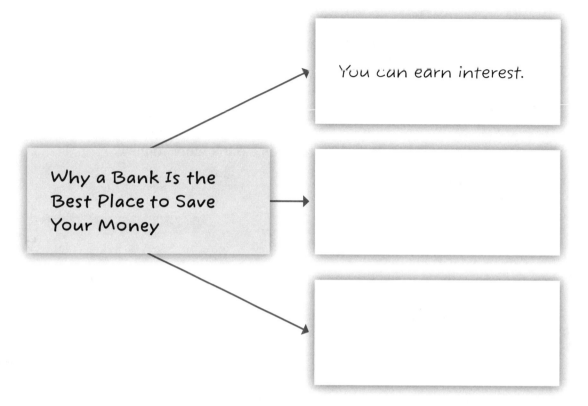

You can earn interest.

Why a Bank Is the Best Place to Save Your Money

**7** Name three places the article suggests someone might save money at home.

_____

**8** According to the article, why might businesses borrow money from banks?

_____

**9** How do people pay the money they borrow back to the bank?

_____

_____

**10** List two ways you can be sure that a bank will return your money to you.

a _____

b _____

# Writing Connection: Pronouns

A **pronoun** is a word that can take the place of a noun. Pronouns like **I**, **you**, **she**, **he**, **it**, **we**, and **they** can be subjects of a sentence. Pronouns like **me**, **you**, **her**, **him**, **it**, **us**, and **them** can be the object of a verb in the sentence. For example:

**That man works at the bank. He is very good with people.**

**The teacher walks toward the children. The teacher greets them.**

**1. Complete the sentence with the correct pronoun.**

In order to buy a new car, Kelly saved for _____ .   **it, them**

_____ can easily withdraw money from your bank account.   **You, Her**

Juan opened a new savings account, which made _____ happy.   **his, him**

The banker answered the questions _____ asked.   **them, we**

**2. Circle the pronoun in each sentence.**

We deposited the money in the bank.

A bank safely stores money for them.

He always saves money.

You borrow money to fix up the house.

I can earn interest quickly.

You should try not to spend it foolishly.

**3. Write two sentences using pronouns about saving money at a bank. Circle the pronouns.**

a _____

_____

b _____

_____

# Saving Lives

Nora woke to the sound of the bell ringing loudly. She jumped out of bed, pulled on her boots, and hurried to the pole. Down she slid to the first floor of the firehouse. She grabbed her hat and coat and got in the truck. More firefighters were close behind. She heard the chief yell, "We'll need four of you on this job!" The truck raced out of the station and down the street. Lights were flashing and the siren was roaring.

The fire was across town. "An old building went up in flames," said Dan. "I wonder how it started."

When the truck got to the fire, Bill shouted, "I'll connect the hoses." He and Nora pulled hoses from the truck to nearby hydrants. Dan and Hank grabbed axes and ran inside to start fighting the fire.

Nora took a hose and went inside the building. There were flames and smoke everywhere, but Nora's mask, hat, coat, and boots helped protect her. She pointed her hose at the fire nearest her. Water streamed out, dousing the flames.

Meanwhile, Hank and Dan searched for people who might be trapped inside. There was no one inside the building. But there were people living in houses next to it. Thankfully there were no injuries.

With Nora and the team working together, it took a few hours to put out the fire. Nora, Dan, Bill, and Hank breathed a sigh of relief. "Another day of saving lives," said Nora. "I love my job!"

**What is the story mostly about?**

_____

Comprehension Matters, Level D    © Options Publishing. No copying permitted.

# Multiple-Choice Questions

**1** Another title for this story could be

Ⓐ "The Ringing Bell."

Ⓑ "Nora's Long Week."

Ⓒ "A Firefighting Team."

Ⓓ "Dan Works Hard."

**2** Who connected the hoses to the hydrant?

Ⓐ Nora

Ⓑ Dan

Ⓒ Bill

Ⓓ Hank

**3** Which of the following did *not* protect Nora from the flames and smoke?

Ⓐ glasses

Ⓑ mask

Ⓒ hat

Ⓓ boots

**4** This story is mostly about firefighters who

Ⓐ fight fires alone.

Ⓑ work together as a team.

Ⓒ don't care for each other.

Ⓓ are not hard workers.

**5** According to the story, how many people were injured in the fire?

Ⓐ three

Ⓑ two

Ⓒ one

Ⓓ zero

# Short-Response Questions

**6** Complete the chart with the missing details.

| Firefighters Work Together | |
|---|---|
| **Action** | **Firefighter(s)** |
| Pulled hoses to _____ | Bill, Nora |
| Connected hoses | |
| Used axes | Dan, Hank |
| Used hose | |
| Searched _____ for people | Dan, Hank |

**7** According to the story, what was Nora doing when she heard the fire bell?

_____

**8** Name two things Nora did to get ready for the fire.

_____

**9** Explain why it is important for firefighters to work together.

_____

_____

**10** List equipment that protects a firefighter.

_____

_____

Comprehension Matters, Level D    © Options Publishing. No copying permitted.

# Writing Connection: Adjectives

An **adjective** is a word that describes a noun.

Here are some sentences with the adjectives and nouns marked.

**An old building went up in flames.**

    adjective    noun

**Gene took the long, sharp axe into the burning house.**

    adjective  adjective  noun

1. **Underline the adjective(s) in each sentence.**

   As she slept, Nora heard the loud bell.

   Ryan pulled on his black boots.

   They pulled the hoses to the leaping flames.

   Strong sprays of water streamed out of the hoses.

   She ran to put on her heavy, fireproof coat.

   Nora grabbed her red helmet and got in the truck.

   The four firefighters rode in a speeding truck.

   The thick smoke blocked everyone's view.

   Thankfully there were no serious injuries.

2. **Write two sentences with correct adjectives about the firefighters in this story.**

   a _____

   _____

   b _____

   _____

# It's in the Mail

Have you ever mailed a letter yourself? If yes, you know that you need to put a postage stamp on the envelope. In the United States, people have been using stamps to send mail for more than 150 years. Before that, sending mail was often free. The people who got the mail had to pay. If you wrote to a friend, the friend would have to pay when the letter got there.

The first official U.S. stamps came out in 1847. This changed everything. People had to pay for delivery ahead of time. They did this by buying stamps. Each stamp cost five cents. One stamp paid for a letter to go up to 300 miles.

The first stamps had to be cut from a big sheet with a pair of scissors. Ten years later, stamps began to be printed on special paper. The paper had tiny holes that made it easy to tear off the stamps. Today stamps are printed like stickers. People can peel them off and stick them on an envelope.

There are all kinds of stamps. You can get them in sheets, books, and rolls. Some have flags, flowers, or even cartoon characters on them. Many people like stamps so much that they collect them.

After the arrival of the Internet, many people stopped sending letters in the mail. However, there are many other things that still get mailed. People often send greeting cards, packages, payments, and other important documents in the mail. The Postal Service delivers over 200 billion pieces of mail per year. Whatever you mail, you still need to put a postage stamp on it. Without postage, the mail will not go anywhere.

**What is the article mostly about?**

_____

# Multiple-Choice Questions

**1** Another title for this article could be

Ⓐ "The Cost of Postage."

Ⓑ "Collecting Stamps."

Ⓒ "All About Stamps."

Ⓓ "How to Mail a Letter."

**2** According to the article, what made some people stop sending letters in the mail?

Ⓐ the cost of postage

Ⓑ printing stamps on special paper

Ⓒ having to buy stamps

Ⓓ the arrival of the Internet

**3** How long have people in the U.S. been using stamps?

Ⓐ 150 years

Ⓑ more than 150 years

Ⓒ less than 150 years

Ⓓ 300 years

**4** What is the fourth paragraph *mostly* about?

Ⓐ different kinds of stamps

Ⓑ collecting stamps

Ⓒ buying stamps

Ⓓ flag stamps

**5** Which sentence from the article *best* supports the idea that we still need post offices today?

Ⓐ In the United States, people have been using stamps to send mail for more than 150 years.

Ⓑ After the arrival of the Internet, many people stopped sending letters in the mail.

Ⓒ People send cards, packages, payments, and other important documents in the mail.

Ⓓ Without postage, the mail will not go anywhere.

# Short-Response Questions

**6** Complete the web with two details.

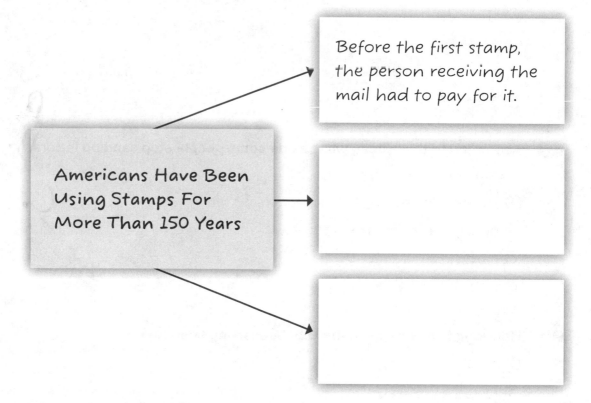

Before the first stamp, the person receiving the mail had to pay for it.

Americans Have Been Using Stamps For More Than 150 Years

**7** According to the article, how were the first stamps printed?

_____

**8** Name two ways stamps are sold.

_____

**9** Why must you put postage on a letter?

_____

_____

**10** List two things that can be printed on stamps.

_____

_____

# Writing Connection: Adverbs

An **adverb** is a word that describes a verb. Here are some sentences with the verbs and adverbs marked.

**Caleb <u>ran</u> <u>quickly</u> to the mailbox.**
    verb    adverb

**She <u>mails</u> our birthday cards <u>early</u>.**
    verb                        adverb

1. **Circle the adverbs and underline the verbs.**

   I open all my letters quickly.

   My friends promptly write me back.

   Mail was delivered slowly many years ago.

   Did you eagerly wait for my note?

   Stamp collectors carefully place their stamps in albums.

2. **Complete the sentence with the correct adverb.**

   A stamp should be placed on a letter _____.   **carelessly, carefully**

   You can _____ mail a letter using a stamp.   **easily, hardly**

   A mail carrier will _____ deliver a letter that has a stamp on it.   **gladly, sadly**

   _____ forgetting to put a stamp on a letter will delay it.   **Carefully, Carelessly**

3. **Write two sentences using adverbs about sending and receiving mail.**

   a _____

   _____

   b _____

   _____

# The Flight of the Golden Plover

Dr. Raquel Ramirez is a biologist who studies bird migration patterns for the state wildlife department. Our reporter, Mica Dwayne, interviewed her about a bird that flies through our state every year.

**DWAYNE:** What kind of bird is the golden plover?

**DR. RAMIREZ:** The golden plover is a shore bird, but you won't find it on the beach. It nests in the grass close by.

**DWAYNE:** What is special about the golden plover?

**DR. RAMIREZ:** The plover flies farther than almost any bird. Each year it takes a trip that starts in South America and ends in the Arctic, at the top of the world.

**DWAYNE:** How can a bird fly that far?

**DR. RAMIREZ:** It's pretty amazing! For a bird to make such a long flight, you would think it must be big and strong. The plover *is* strong, but it is not big. A full-grown plover is about the size of a robin, which is a small bird. It weighs less than half a pound and is shorter than a standard ruler. To make that long flight, the plover stops every so often. It rests and eats bugs and worms to give it strength to keep going. The plover can reach a flight speed of up to 60 miles per hour.

**DWAYNE:** Can you tell me more about its flight?

**DR. RAMIREZ:** Sure. The plover flies over both countries and oceans. It flies over Peru, Colombia, and a strip of land in Mexico. Then the plover flies over the Gulf of Mexico and crosses Texas on its journey through the states. By the start of summer, this strong bird is far north, in the Arctic. Here the bird stops, but only for the summer. Then what does it do? It turns around and heads south!

**What is the interview mostly about?**

_____

# Multiple-Choice Questions

**1** Another title for this article could be

Ⓐ "Big Bird, Big Flight."

Ⓑ "Plovers Don't Fly."

Ⓒ "A Shore Bird."

Ⓓ "Small Bird, Big Flight."

**2** Where does a golden plover build its nest?

Ⓐ on the shore

Ⓑ in a tree

Ⓒ on the beach

Ⓓ in the grass near the beach

**3** How fast can a golden plover fly?

Ⓐ up to 20 miles per hour

Ⓑ up to 40 miles per hour

Ⓒ up to 60 miles per hour

Ⓓ up to 80 miles per hour

**4** Which detail *best* supports the idea that the golden plover is a strong bird?

Ⓐ the plover's size

Ⓑ the plover's long flight

Ⓒ the plover's nest

Ⓓ the plover's diet

**5** Which of the following places is *not* visited by a golden plover?

Ⓐ Germany

Ⓑ South America

Ⓒ Texas

Ⓓ Mexico

# Short-Response Questions

**6** Complete the diagram with details from the article.

> 1. Starts flight in South America

> 2. Flies over Peru, _____, and Mexico

> 3. Flies over the Gulf of Mexico and crosses _____

> 4.

**7** According to the article, what does the golden plover eat?

_____

**8** Describe the size of a golden plover.

_____

**9** Why might you think that the golden plover is a big bird?

_____

_____

**10** List two places that are included in the plover's flight.

_____

_____

Comprehension Matters, Level D    © Options Publishing. No copying permitted.

# Writing Connection: Subject-Verb Agreement

In a sentence, **subjects** and **verbs** must agree in number. If the subject is singular, the verb must be singular. If the subject is plural, the verb must be plural. Here are some sentences with the subjects and verbs marked.

**The golden plover is a shore bird.**
  singular subject   singular verb

**Golden plovers are shore birds.**
  plural subject   plural verb

1. **Complete the sentence with the correct verb form.**

   The plover _____ a busy bird.   **are, is**

   Golden plovers _____ not big birds.   **are, is**

   A plover actually _____ very little.   **weigh, weighs**

   The bird _____ in the Arctic during the summer.   **lives, live**

2. **Circle the subject and verb in each sentence. Then identify the subject and verb as *S* for singular or *P* for plural.**

   Golden plovers take long trips each year.   _____

   The plover can reach a flight speed of up to 60 miles per hour.   _____

   A plover is a small bird.   _____

   Far above the ground, the plover flies over land and water.   _____

   The nest of a plover is found in the grass.   _____

   After a plover rests for the summer, it turns around and flies south.   _____

3. **Write two sentences with correct subject-verb agreement about golden plovers.**

   a _____

   _____

   b _____

   _____

# Spring Concert

Callie and Nick were going to sing a song together at the spring concert. They had practiced hard for weeks. But Nick was nervous.

Mr. Barnes was their music teacher. He was helping them get ready for the concert. The day before the concert, Nick talked with Mr. Barnes. He told him he didn't think he could sing.

"Do you think you know the song?" asked Mr. Barnes. Nick nodded his head. Mr. Barnes asked another question. "Do you like to sing?"

Nick answered, "Very much."

Mr. Barnes explained that Nick might be nervous. Nick agreed. The kind teacher told Nick that even famous singers get nervous before a show. Nick felt a little better and decided to try.

The next night Nick was still nervous. He wondered if he would start singing on time. He thought he might forget the words. He worried he might trip while walking on stage. Callie said she was nervous, too. "But I know we can do it, Nick," she said.

Mr. Barnes introduced them to the audience. Callie and Nick smiled as they walked on stage. The audience was quiet as the piano played. When it came time for Nick's part, he began to sing. Before he knew it, the song was over. The audience was smiling and clapping.

Nick was very proud of himself. The next day he saw Mr. Barnes. "It was hard to go on stage," he said. "But it was worth it!"

**What is the story mostly about?**

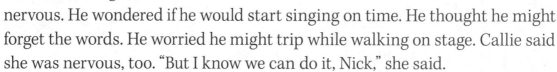

# Multiple-Choice Questions

**1** **Another title for this article could be**

Ⓐ "Stage Fright."

Ⓑ "Nick Forgets the Words."

Ⓒ "Callie is Nervous."

Ⓓ "Mr. Barnes."

**2** **According to the story, how did Nick feel before he sang?**

Ⓐ excited

Ⓑ nervous

Ⓒ sad

Ⓓ angry

**3** **What time of day did the concert take place?**

Ⓐ morning

Ⓑ afternoon

Ⓒ night

Ⓓ late afternoon

**4** **What did Nick think the day after he sang?**

Ⓐ He shouldn't have done it.

Ⓑ He was still nervous.

Ⓒ It didn't go well.

Ⓓ It was worth it.

**5** **How did Nick feel after the concert?**

Ⓐ scared

Ⓑ angry

Ⓒ proud

Ⓓ sad

# Short-Response Questions

**6** Complete the web with two details.

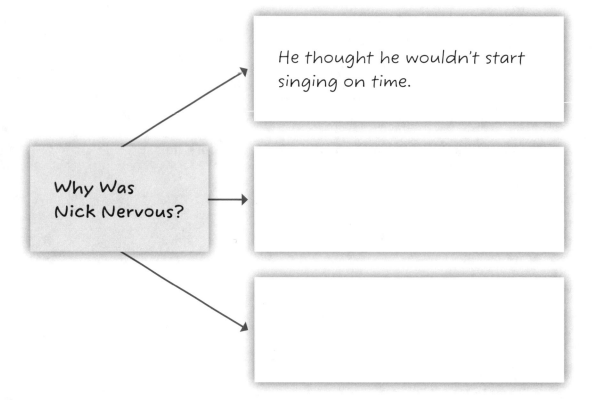

He thought he wouldn't start singing on time.

Why Was Nick Nervous?

**7** How did Mr. Barnes help Nick?

_____

**8** How long did Nick and Callie practice for the concert?

_____

**9** How did Callie help Nick?

_____

_____

**10** How did Nick and Callie know they did a good job?

_____

_____

Comprehension Matters, Level D

# Writing Connection: Conjunctions

A **conjunction** is a word that joins two sentences together. Some words that are used as conjunctions are **and**, **or**, **but**, **yet**, and **so**. Here are two examples.

**The concert started at noon. We arrived late.**
**The concert started at noon, <u>but</u> we arrived late.**

**The kids sang well. The crowd cheered.**
**The kids sang well, <u>so</u> the crowd cheered.**

**1. Underline the conjunction in each sentence.**

Nick was performing in the spring concert, and he was nervous.

Nick thought he might forget the words, but he sang the song well.

Nick could have dropped out of the concert, or he could have tried his best.

Nick decided he would sing, so he was very proud of himself.

**2. Complete the sentences with the correct conjunctions.**

The sisters were going to sing together, _____ they practiced a lot.   **so, but**

The spring concert is coming up soon, _____ we are going to it.   **yet, and**

We sold 300 tickets, _____ the theater was crowded.   **or, so**

Let's leave now, _____ we'll be late!   **but, or**

**3. Write two sentences with conjunctions about the story. Circle the conjunction.**

a _____

_____

b _____

_____

# A New Zoo View

Now there is a new way to visit a zoo. And you don't have to go very far. Many zoos are putting video cameras in their animal areas. These are called "animal cams." They are placed with giant pandas, tigers, and polar bears. They are also put with elephants, apes, penguins, and sharks.

The video cameras are connected to the Internet. This allows anyone to visit zoos located nearby and far away. Go to your public library, school, or home computer and use the Internet. From there, you can go to the zoo. Watch a giant

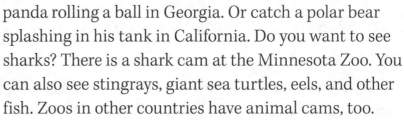

PANDA CAM

panda rolling a ball in Georgia. Or catch a polar bear splashing in his tank in California. Do you want to see sharks? There is a shark cam at the Minnesota Zoo. You can also see stingrays, giant sea turtles, eels, and other fish. Zoos in other countries have animal cams, too.

Animal lovers from all over the world watch animal cams. Internet zoo visits are very popular. It's easy to see why. You don't have to pay for a ticket. And you don't have to wait in line to see the animals. Some animal cams even allow you to control the camera. You can zoom in for a closer look. Or make the camera change direction.

Zoos record how many people watch their animal cams. These numbers tell how popular they are. Zoo Atlanta knows that 50,000 people watch their panda cam every day! Internet visitors watch the giant panda cub, Mei Lan, as she plays, eats, and sleeps.

You can ask your teacher or parent to help you search for zoo animal cams on the Internet. Then watch from your computer as the animals eat, play, swim, swing, or sleep. Get ready for a new zoo view!

**What is the article mostly about?**

_____

34

# Multiple-Choice Questions

**1** **Another title for this article could be**

Ⓐ "Polar Bear Splash."

Ⓑ "My Favorite Panda, Mei Lan."

Ⓒ "Zoo Animal Cams: Bringing the Zoo to You."

Ⓓ "Small Town Zoos are the Best."

**2** **Which statement *best* supports the idea that animal cams are popular?**

Ⓐ Watch the Shark Cam at a Minnesota zoo.

Ⓑ See a polar bear splashing in his tank in San Diego, California.

Ⓒ There are animal cams in zoos in other countries, too.

Ⓓ Every day 50,000 Internet viewers watch Zoo Atlanta's panda cam.

**3** **How are people able to view the animal cams?**

Ⓐ They go to a zoo and watch a special screen.

Ⓑ They use the Internet.

Ⓒ They go to a movie theater in their town.

Ⓓ They order a video from the zoo.

**4** **What is the first paragraph mostly about?**

Ⓐ zoo tickets

Ⓑ long lines

Ⓒ animal cams

Ⓓ polar bears

**5** **According to the article, what animal from Zoo Atlanta is watched daily by thousands of animal cam viewers?**

Ⓐ Taz, the western lowland gorilla

Ⓑ Farasi, the African lion

Ⓒ Bamboo, the red panda

Ⓓ Mei Lan, the giant panda cub

## Short-Response Questions

**6** Complete the web with two details.

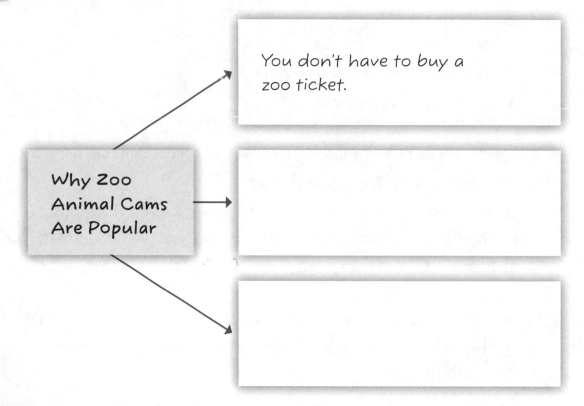

You don't have to buy a zoo ticket.

Why Zoo Animal Cams Are Popular

**7** Where can you go to use a computer to "visit" a zoo?

_____

**8** According to the article, which zoo has a shark cam?

_____

**9** What tells how popular a zoo animal cam is?

_____

_____

**10** Name five animals that can be seen on an animal cam.

_____

_____

# Writing Connection: Sentences

A **complete sentence** contains a subject and a verb. The subject can be a noun or pronoun. The subject is what the sentence is about. The verb is what happens to the subject or what the subject does.

Here are some complete sentences with the subjects and verbs marked.

**Penguins swim in the coldest ocean currents.**
subject    verb

**They depend on their feathers and layers of fat to keep warm.**
subject    verb

1. **Underline the subject and circle the verb in each sentence.**

    The penguin's feathers form a warm outer coat.

    They live in colonies with hundreds of other penguins.

    The rockhopper penguin bounces up to 5 feet high.

    Some penguin nests are made of rocks.

    We controlled the penguin cam on the school computer.

    The penguin keeper fed the penguins fish in the morning.

    A penguin ate a fish in one gulp!

    We saw penguins "flying" underwater.

    They even played diving games.

2. **Write two complete sentences that tell about animal cams.**

    a _____

    _____

    b _____

    _____

# Keisha and the Amazing Markers

Keisha yawned. She did not want to get out of bed. "At least it's Friday," she thought. Tomorrow was Saturday, and she was looking forward to spending the whole day drawing with her new markers.

That week, Keisha's dad had taken a business trip. When he came home, he had a surprise for her—a new set of markers from an art store! They were not like any markers Keisha had seen before. Her dad said these were the kind that real artists use. Keisha wanted to be a real artist more than anything. When she

wasn't in school or doing homework, she was drawing. Drawing seemed to take her away to another place.

Keisha put her markers in her bag. She wanted to show them to her art teacher. As she got on the bus, her backpack began to shake. Keisha sat down and took it off. The pack opened, and all of the markers jumped out.

Keisha's mouth dropped open. She and the other kids watched as the markers started drawing pictures in the air. One marker drew a picture of the Alamo in Texas. Another drew the White House in Washington, D.C.

Keisha could not believe her eyes! This time, drawing really *was* taking her to another place! She stared as the markers kept drawing. She saw the Grand Canyon, the Sears Tower, and the Empire State Building. These were all places she would like to visit someday.

The bus came to a stop in front of the school. As the doors opened, Keisha jerked awake. She was still in her bed. It was just a dream! She sat up and looked at the markers on her dresser. One of them was out of the package. There was a picture lying next to it. It was a drawing of the Sears Tower!

**What is the story mostly about?**

_____

# Multiple-Choice Questions

**1** **Another title for this article could be**

Ⓐ "I Love Markers."

Ⓑ "A Day at School."

Ⓒ "Magic Pictures."

Ⓓ "Sleeping In."

**2** **What is Keisha's favorite activity?**

Ⓐ sleeping

Ⓑ drawing

Ⓒ going to school

Ⓓ going on trips

**3** **According to the story, why did Keisha bring her markers to school?**

Ⓐ to show them to her dad

Ⓑ to show them to the bus driver

Ⓒ to show them to other kids

Ⓓ to show them to her art teacher

**4** **What is the first paragraph *mostly* about?**

Ⓐ Keisha looks forward to trying out her new markers.

Ⓑ Keisha draws more pictures.

Ⓒ Keisha doesn't like the new markers.

Ⓓ Keisha wakes up from her dream.

**5** **Which of the following places is *not* mentioned in the story?**

Ⓐ the Alamo

Ⓑ the Golden Gate Bridge

Ⓒ the White House

Ⓓ the Sears Tower

## Short-Response Questions

**6** Complete the chart with two details.

| Keisha's Dream |
|---|
| 1. The markers jump out of her backpack. |
| 2. |
| 3. |
| 4. She wakes up. |

**7** According to the story, what was special about the places in the drawings?

_____

**8** Name three details in the story that helped you figure out it was not real.

a _____

b _____

c _____

**9** What does Keisha want to be someday?

_____

_____

**10** Which detail at the beginning of the story tells you that Keisha's dad was thinking of her while he was on his trip?

_____

_____

Comprehension Matters, Level D   © Options Publishing. No copying permitted.

# Writing Connection: Clauses

A **complex sentence** is made up of an independent clause and one or more dependent clauses. An **independent clause** can be used on its own. It is a sentence with a subject and a verb.

A **dependent clause** cannot be used on its own. Although it has a subject and a verb, it sounds incomplete on its own. Here is an example of a complex sentence.

**José and Lupe went to the movies**     **after they finished studying.**

independent clause                              dependent clause

José and Lupe went to the movies can be used alone as a sentence. It is an independent clause.

After they finished studying sounds incomplete on its own. It is a dependent clause.

1. **Underline the independent clause and circle the dependent clause in each sentence.**

   Keisha was tired when she woke up.

   Keisha's dad gave her some markers after he returned from a trip.

   She was excited to get the markers because she wants to be an artist.

   Keisha spent her time drawing when she wasn't in school.

2. **Write two complex sentences about Keisha's dream.**

   a _____

   _____

   b _____

   _____

# A Basket of Pollen

### Introduction

When you think of bees, you might picture busy hives and honey, flowers, or stingers. Maybe we should think about baskets of pollen. Bees have their own little baskets in which they carry pollen. This is very important to nature and to us. Why?

### Bees in Action

A careful look at bees in action will tell us. Bees fly from one flower to another looking for two things—nectar and pollen. Nectar is a food that gives bees energy. It is also what bees use to make honey. Pollen is a food that helps bees grow and stay strong. Bees need nectar and pollen to live.

Different kinds of bees get nectar and pollen in different ways. But one thing is common among female honey bees. They have something on their legs that no other insects have. It's a pollen basket. The basket is made of stiff hairs. When the bee visits a flower, she pushes pollen into the basket, and some of it also sticks to the hairs. Then she carries the pollen back to the hive.

Pollen falls off the bees' legs when they visit other flowers. That means they take pollen from one flower and drop it into another. Though this seems like an accident, it is an important step in helping new flowers grow.

### The Key to Life

For plants, pollen is the key to life. If pollen was not moved from one flower to another, plants would die out. If plants died out, people would die out, too. We need plants for food, clean air, and clean water. Bees help move pollen, so they help people and plants live. The next time you see a bee, say "Thank you!"

**What is the article mostly about?**

_____

_____

# Multiple-Choice Questions

**1** **Another title for this web page could be**

Ⓐ "Why We Need Bees."

Ⓑ "Bees Eat Nectar."

Ⓒ "Bees' Knees."

Ⓓ "Bees Fly Around."

**2** **What is a pollen basket made of?**

Ⓐ pieces of wood

Ⓑ metal

Ⓒ hair and fur

Ⓓ stiff hairs

**3** **According to the web page, what kind of bees have a pollen basket?**

Ⓐ male honey bees

Ⓑ female leaf-cutting bees

Ⓒ female honey bees

Ⓓ male leaf-cutting bees

**4** **What is the last paragraph *mostly* about?**

Ⓐ how bees fly from flower to flower

Ⓑ how bees get pollen

Ⓒ how bees help plants and people

Ⓓ how bees get nectar

**5** **What is nectar?**

Ⓐ food that helps bees grow and stay strong

Ⓑ food that gives bees energy

Ⓒ food that helps bees gather pollen

Ⓓ food that gives bees their color

# Short-Response Questions

**6** Complete the web with two details.

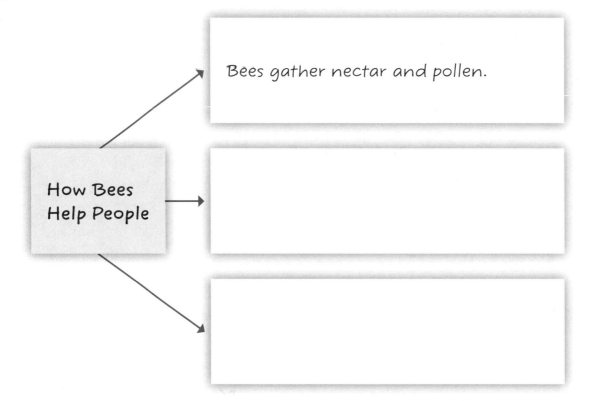

Bees gather nectar and pollen.

How Bees Help People

**7** According to the article, which process seems like an accident?

_____

**8** Name two things bees are looking for in flowers.

_____

**9** Why do people need plants?

_____

_____

**10** List two things you might picture when you think of bees.

a _____

b _____

# Writing Connection: Prepositional Phrases

**Prepositions** link nouns, pronouns, or groups of words in a sentence.
They show when, where, or how two things are connected.

The noun or pronoun that follows a preposition is called its **object.**
**A prepositional phrase** is made up of a preposition plus its object.

Some prepositions are **of, at, in, on, to, up,** and **by**.

He brought the flowers *before* breakfast.  (When did he bring them?)

The flower is growing *under* a tree.  (Where is it growing?)

He bought some honey *with* his money.  (How did he buy it?)

1.  **Underline the prepositional phrase in each sentence.**

We planted flowers in the front yard.

They should bloom more after spring.

What would we do without their colors?

The garden store clerk put the plants on the table.

They will grow with water and sunlight.

Wendy saw bees in the flowers.

My watering can is near the tomato plants.

Thank the bees when you walk through the garden.

2.  **Write two sentences with prepositional phrases about bees. Circle each preposition.**

a _____

_____

b _____

_____

# How to Take Care of Your Eyes

It is important to take good care of your eyes. Here are some tips.

First, have a doctor check your eyes every year. An eye doctor can make sure your eyes are healthy and you are seeing clearly. Eye exams do not take long, and they do not hurt. However, some parts of the exam can be uncomfortable because you may not be used to them. Wear eyeglasses or contact lenses if the doctor thinks that you need them.

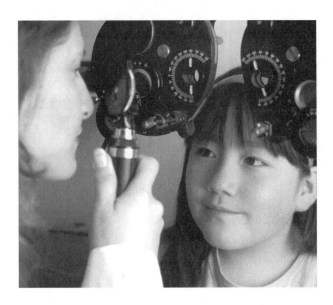

Second, eat right, exercise, and sleep. Drink plenty of milk and water, and eat fruits and vegetables. Give your body enough rest each night. Eyes that are well-rested are able to work better.

Last, never look directly into the sun. Light comes into the eye through the pupil. The eyes are made to see only certain types of light. Direct sun is too bright for the eyes to handle. Wear sunglasses on bright days.

Make sure there is plenty of light when you read. Do not sit too close to the television or computer screen.

Your eyes are the only pair you have. Take care of them, and they will help take care of you!

**What is the article mostly about?**

_____

_____

# Multiple-Choice Questions

**1**   **Another title for this article could be**

   Ⓐ "Seeing An Eye Doctor."

   Ⓑ "The Sun Is Bright."

   Ⓒ "Protecting Your Vision."

   Ⓓ "Eat Right."

**2**   **Eye exams**

   Ⓐ are not important.

   Ⓑ really hurt.

   Ⓒ take a long time.

   Ⓓ do not hurt.

**3**   **According to the article, how often should an eye doctor check your eyes?**

   Ⓐ each day

   Ⓑ each year

   Ⓒ each month

   Ⓓ each hour

**4**   **What is the second paragraph *mostly* about?**

   Ⓐ why it's important to take care of your eyes

   Ⓑ using your eyes every day

   Ⓒ having an eye doctor check your eyes

   Ⓓ what kinds of foods can help your eyes

**5**   **Which of the following actions is *not* good for your eyes?**

   Ⓐ get an eye exam

   Ⓑ look at the sun

   Ⓒ eat right

   Ⓓ exercise

# Short-Response Questions

**6** Complete the chart with two details.

| Ways to Take Care of Your Eyes |
| --- |
| A. Get an eye exam each year. |
| B. |
| C. |

**7** According to the article, why should you get plenty of rest?

_____

_____

**8** Name two beverages you should drink often for healthy eyes.

_____

**9** After reading this article, write why it's important to take care of your eyes.

_____

_____

**10** List two ways to take care of your eyes at home.

_____

_____

Comprehension Matters Level D    © Options Publishing. No copying permitted.

# Writing Connection: Adjectives

A **comparative adjective** compares two things. It is formed by adding **-er** to the adjective. A **superlative adjective** compares three or more things. It is formed by adding **-est** to the adjective.

**The flashlight is <u>brighter</u> than the candle's light.**
                     comparative adjective

**The lamplight is the <u>brightest</u> light in the house.**
                   superlative adjective

1. **Complete the sentence with the correct adjective.**

   The sun is the _____ star in our sky, and it can harm your eyes if you look directly at it.  **brighter, brightest**

   Taking care of your eyes is no _____ than anything else you do for your body.  **harder, hardest**

   One of the _____ things you can do is to choose healthful foods.  **easier, easiest**

   Contact lenses are _____ than eyeglass lenses.  **thinner, thinnest**

2. **Circle the comparative or superlative adjective in each sentence. Then identify the adjective as *C* for comparative or *S* for superlative.**

   Your glasses are a brighter color than mine.  _____

   I had to wait longer for my mom to get her eyes checked.  _____

   Those glasses are the coolest that I've ever seen!  _____

   It's easier for me to see when I wear my glasses.  _____

3. **Write two sentences about the eyes and use a comparative or superlative adjective in each sentence.**

   a _____

   _____

   b _____

   _____

# The Mystery of the Crooked Box Lid

My grandma loves family photos! She calls them pictures. She even has some from when she was a girl. Grandma keeps most of her pictures in boxes that she arranged by date. They are lined up on a shelf in her living room.

I wanted to surprise her on Grandparents Day with something special. I told Mom my idea. She said she would help me borrow some of the pictures. So we made a plan.

Mom and I took a cake to Grandma that day. Later, Mom asked me to serve the cake while she and Grandma sat outside. That was my signal. I opened one of the picture boxes. I took out pictures of Grandma with her parents. I knew these pictures were extra special to her. I put the box back on the shelf as carefully as I could.

Mom and Grandma were having tea the next day. Grandma asked Mom if it seemed like something was different in the room. "Hmm," Mom said as she looked around. "Seems fine to me."

Grandma finally said, "That picture box lid isn't straight."

"Mother," said my mom, "maybe you moved it when you were dusting."

Mom is a fast thinker! While they were visiting, I was at the store making large copies of Grandma's pictures. On Grandparents Day, I surprised Grandma. When she opened the photo album, she started to cry. "So now I know why a certain box lid was crooked!" she said with a laugh.

"I had to borrow some of them," I explained. "I wanted to surprise you."

"Larry, you sure did!" Grandma said as she hugged me.

**What is the story mostly about?**

_____

# Multiple-Choice Questions

**1** **Another title for this story could be**

(A) "A Surprise for Grandma."

(B) "Mom's Photos."

(C) "Making Copies."

(D) "Going to Grandma's."

**2** **Where did Grandma keep her photos?**

(A) in albums

(B) in boxes

(C) on her computer

(D) on a bulletin board

**3** **What was Larry's signal to look for photos?**

(A) His mom asked him to serve cake.

(B) His mom cleared her throat.

(C) He heard a bell ring.

(D) The door slammed shut.

**4** **Which detail shows how happy Grandma was with her surprise?**

(A) She grinned at Larry.

(B) She started to cry.

(C) She gave Larry a big kiss.

(D) She jumped for joy.

**5** **Larry gave Grandma her surprise on**

(A) Mother's Day.

(B) her birthday.

(C) Christmas.

(D) Grandparents Day.

# Short-Response Questions

**6** Complete the web with two details.

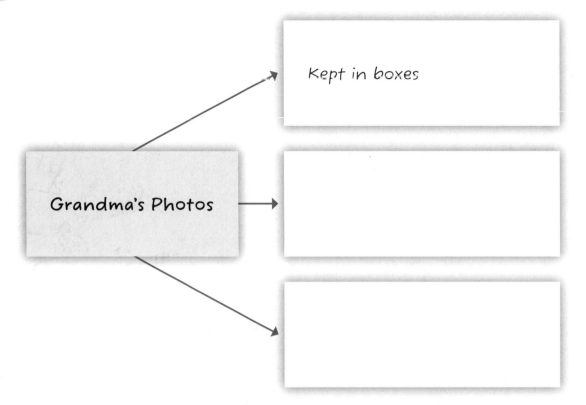

Kept in boxes

Grandma's Photos

**7** Where was Grandma when Larry borrowed her pictures?

_____

**8** Name two people that were in Grandma's photos.

_____

**9** Why did Larry and his mom make a plan to borrow some of Grandma's photos?

_____

_____

**10** What mystery did the photo album solve?

_____

_____

# Writing Connection: Possessives

When you want to show that something belongs to a person, place, or thing, you use the **possessive** form of a noun. For most singular nouns, you do this by adding **'s** to the word.

Here are some examples.

**Grandma is <u>Mom's</u> mother.**
possessive form

**I borrowed photos from <u>Grandma's</u> box.**
possessive form

**1.** **Complete the sentence with the correct possessive form.**

_____ pictures were stored in boxes.   **Grandma**

_____ idea was a great one.   **Mom**

I used the _____ copy machine.   **store**

My _____ photo is in a frame on the wall.   **father**

Grandma's cake tastes the best. _____ camera is not new.   **Niko**

Will you help me plan _____ surprise?   **Tyrone**

My _____ camera is in the camera case.   **sister**

Our _____ photo was blurry.   **dog**

**2.** **Write two sentences about the story using possessives correctly.**

a _____

_____

b _____

_____

# Dear Mr. Mike

Dear Mr. Mike,

I am writing to ask you for help. I am in fourth grade, and I am in our school's Green Club. We are trying to think of ways to get volunteers for our schoolyard workday. It happens in two weeks. Last year the club had enough helpers to plant a butterfly garden by the cafeteria. Mrs. Odette is our parent sponsor. She says we will be planting bushes and flowers in front of the school. We'll need lots of volunteers for that.

Our club is worried that we won't have enough helpers. Do you think it is a good idea to make flyers about the workday? Or should we just make posters for the hallway? This project is important to us. Parents' Day is soon. And we want the schoolyard to look its best.

Thank you,
Juan

---

Dear Juan,

The Green Club sounds like a very caring group. Your ideas are good ones. Tell Mrs. Odette about them. Maybe she can get permission from your principal to send a flyer home with each student. Put a photo of the butterfly garden on the flyer. This will let everyone know what can be done when everyone helps. Ask parents to call Mrs. Odette to let her know that she can count on them. You should get plenty of volunteers this way. Remember to thank everyone when they show up!

Take pictures during the workday. Then decorate posters that say " Thank You." Put the posters in the hallway on Parents' Day. It's a nice way to thank the Green Club helpers.

Go, Green Club!
Mr. Mike

# Multiple-Choice Questions

**1** Which sentence *best* states the main idea of the letters?

   Ⓐ People like butterfly gardens more than others.

   Ⓑ Sometimes friends tease each other.

   Ⓒ Being in a club can be fun.

   Ⓓ Talking about problems can help solve them.

**2** Another title for this story could be

   Ⓐ "Juan's Problem with Posters."

   Ⓑ "Advice from Mr. Mike."

   Ⓒ "More Butterflies!"

   Ⓓ "Mrs. Odette."

**3** What does <u>volunteers</u> mean?

   Ⓐ people who offer to help

   Ⓑ Parents' Day visitors

   Ⓒ people who design flyers

   Ⓓ students who belong to clubs

**4** What is the problem in the Green Club?

   Ⓐ They need a lawn mower.

   Ⓑ No one wants to help.

   Ⓒ They need volunteers for a workday.

   Ⓓ Mrs. Odette is quitting the Green Club.

**5** Why does Mr. Mike think the Green Club is caring?

   Ⓐ The club members worry about what to plant.

   Ⓑ The club thanks its helpers.

   Ⓒ The club has a parent sponsor.

   Ⓓ The club wants the schoolyard to look good.

**6** According to the letters, why does the Green Club want volunteers?

Ⓐ to have a car wash

Ⓑ to weed the butterfly garden

Ⓒ to help them plant things

Ⓓ to make flyers

**7** According to Mr. Mike, why should the flyer have a butterfly garden picture?

Ⓐ to show what can be done when people help

Ⓑ to add color to the flyer

Ⓒ to show what a butterfly looks like

Ⓓ to show what a big garden it is

**8** Mr. Mike suggests that Juan

Ⓐ thank the volunteers when they show up.

Ⓑ make sandwiches for everyone.

Ⓒ ask the principal to do all the work.

Ⓓ forget about the workday.

**9** Read the chart. Then write the main idea in the chart.

| Main Idea | Details |
|---|---|
|  | The Green Club wants to make the schoolyard look nice. |
|  | The club worries it will not have much help. |

**10** What is the main idea of the second paragraph of Mr. Mike's letter?

_____

_____